JANE GOODALL

Living with the chimpanzees

Contents

Annie Ortiz • Denise Ferrell

RIGBY

Introduction

Jane Goodall always knew that when she grew up she wanted to work with animals. Her dream was to travel to Africa. Twenty years later her dream came true, when she was working in Africa studying chimpanzees.

Since then she has written lots of books about chimps, and set up a programme for young people all over the world who care about animals and the environment.

Growing Up

Jane Goodall was born in London on 3rd April 1934.

When she was 2, her father gave her a toy chimpanzee, which she called Jubilee.

She was always interested in animals and she loved to read. When she was 7, her grandmother gave her a copy of *The Story of Doctor Dolittle* by Hugh Lofting. Jane loved the book and read it many times. Reading about Doctor Dolittle and his animals inspired her dream of going to Africa.

When she was 10, her grandmother gave her a special present. It was a fully grown tree. Jane liked to sit in the shade of the tree and watch the birds and animals.

Jane holding Jubilee, with her sister and her nanny

Jane started a nature club with her sister and friends. They called it the Alligator Club. The club had a newsletter. It was filled with Jane's drawings and notes about nature.

Learning to Observe

Jane loved exploring the countryside and watching nature. She liked to dig around in the soil and watch the tiny insects she found.

Jane with Uncle Eric's dog

Jane learned a lot about animal behaviour from her dog Rusty. She had fun watching him learn. She saw him solve problems. She believed he had feelings.

Jane and Rusty

Jane's careful observations of Rusty helped her when she finally reached Africa and began to study the wild animals.

Going to Africa

After Jane left school, she moved from job to job. A few years later, a friend invited her to Africa.

Jane worked as a waitress to earn money for her trip. When she had saved enough money, she sailed to Africa. Her dream was coming true!

When Jane got to Africa, she met Dr Louis Leakey, a famous scientist who studied fossils of early humans.

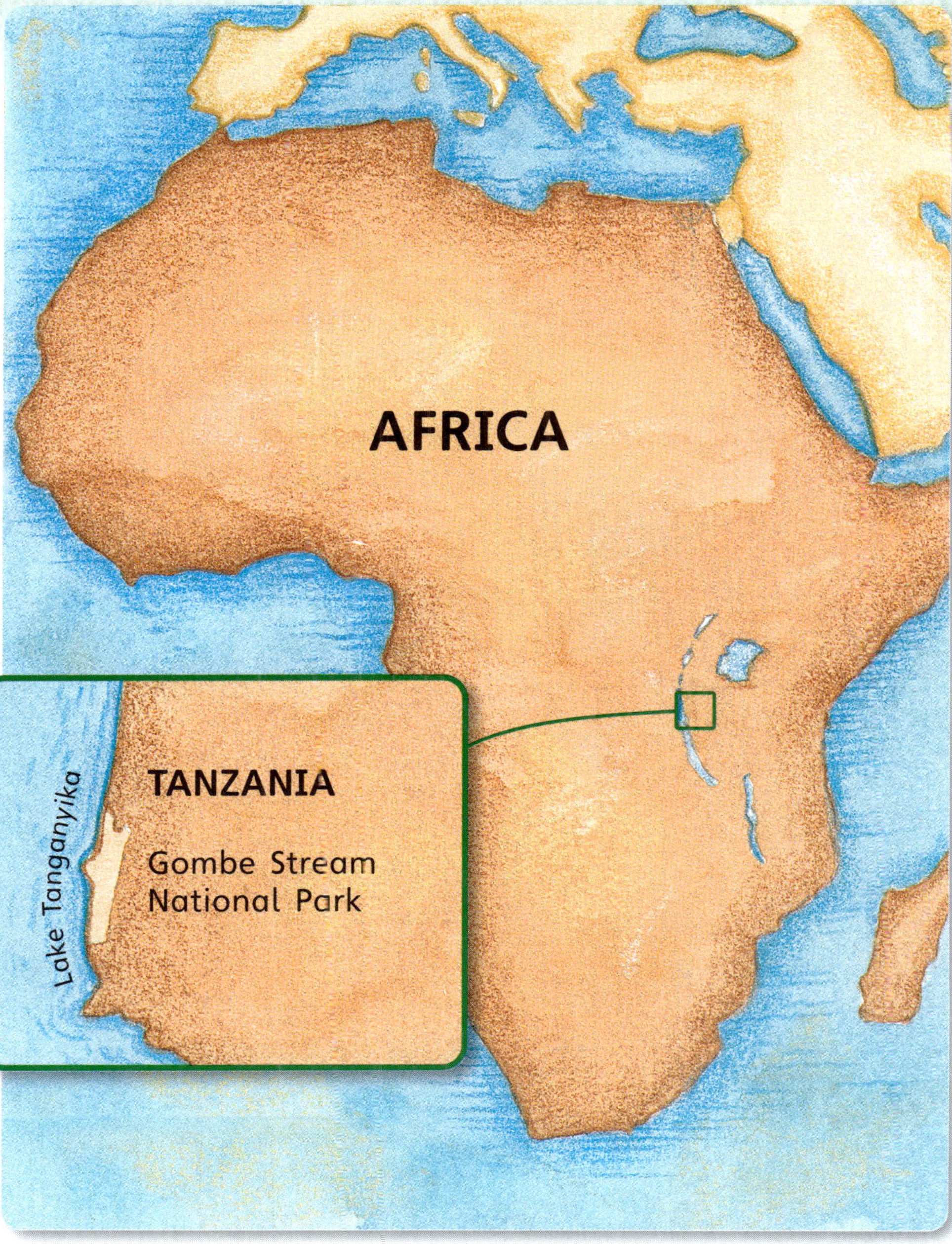
AFRICA
TANZANIA
Gombe Stream
National Park
Lake Tanganyika

Dr Leakey saw that Jane loved animals and wanted to learn more about them. He offered Jane a job.

Jane greets a young chimpanzee.

Dr Leakey asked Jane to observe the chimpanzees and write about them. She set up a camp in Gombe National Park in Tanzania, Africa.

The camp at Gombe National Park

Living with the Chimpanzees

The chimps in the national park were wild and free. They were not Jane's pets. She did not train them. She did not play with them. She just observed them.

Jane saw and heard chimps communicate with each other. They used grunts, pants and hoots. They also hugged, held hands and patted each other.

Meet the Chimps

Unlike other people who studied animals, Jane named each chimp. Here are a few of the many chimpanzees she studied.

David Greybeard was the first chimp to visit Jane's camp and the first to be observed using tools.

Flo was a caring mother and a top-ranking female.

At four years old, Fifi practised at being a mother with young Gilka.

Goliath was the first top-ranking male Jane met.

Mike was a small male chimp who used brains, not size, to be the alpha male.

Jane learned a lot about the chimpanzees she studied. Every night she wrote about them in her journal.

Jane learned that chimps gather and share food.

They live in groups.

They work together to groom each other.

Male chimps are the leaders. The alpha male fights to keep his place.

Jane has been observing chimps for over forty years. No other scientist has ever studied a group of wild animals for such a long time. Her observations are very careful and detailed and she has made several important discoveries.

One discovery was that chimpanzees eat meat.

Another was that chimps use tools.

She also found that each chimp had a different personality.

Her Work Continues

Now Jane travels the world telling people the things she has learned. She also writes books about chimpanzees for children and adults. She has a programme called Roots & Shoots for young people interested in helping animals and the environment. The programme has groups in 68 countries, and many children have become interested in wild life, thanks to Jane's work.

1960
Begins living among chimps

1961
Meets chimps David Greybeard and Flo

1964
Observes Mike as alpha male

1965
Earns Ph.D. in England

1988
Writes her autobiography

1991
Starts Roots & Shoots for young people to help animals

Index

Gardening

how to grow things

A Puffin Book

Written and produced by McPhee Gribble Publishers

Illustrated by David Lancashire

Garden plots

When you start your own garden in the ground or in pots, you will find that you and your plants work together with the soil in a special way.

By watching small plants growing and working in the earth with your hands, you will get to know your garden's needs.

Plants need sunshine, food from the soil and water to grow.

If you have room for a garden plot of your own, choose a place where the plants will get sun for at least half of the day.

Try to find somewhere where water doesn't lie around in puddles. Or mound the soil up and dig gutters to carry extra water away.

Make your garden the right size for you – so you can reach every part without standing on the plants.

If you are starting a plot where no garden has been before, the soil will need a lot of care before you can grow things.

With a garden spade turn the soil over to break it up and let in light and air. A good soaking with water a while before you dig will help if the ground is hard.

If grass and weeds have been growing dig them well under. Pick out any stones.

Use a rake to break the clods into a fine crumbly bed. Level the ground too.

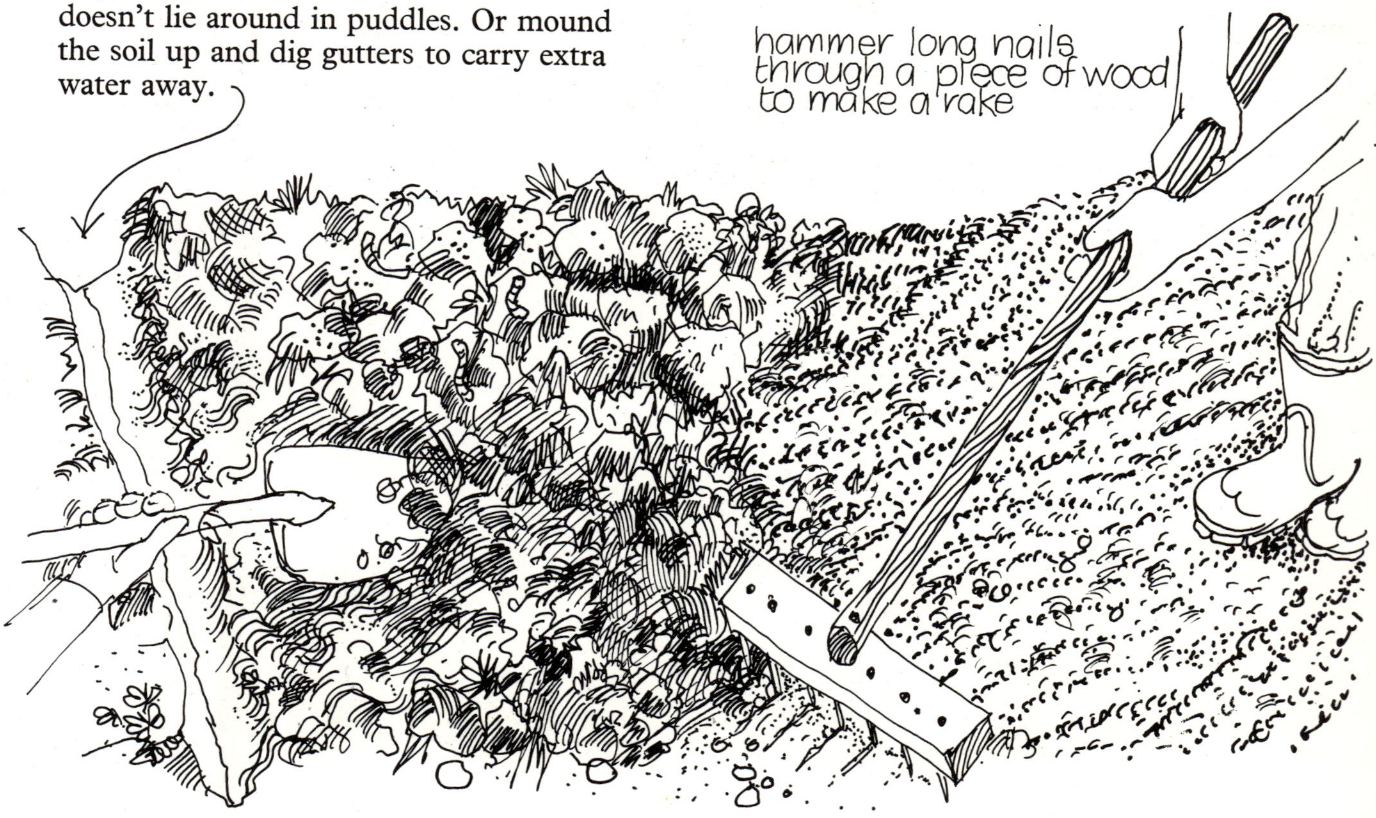

The soil in a new garden will need to be made richer. You can use manure, compost or buy some fertilizer.

Some kinds of animal manure can be mixed with the soil. Cow, horse or chicken manure is best.

Compost is rotted plant matter like vegetable peelings, tea leaves, grass clippings or dead leaves. You could dig a trench at one end of your plot. Cover each pile of scraps with a layer of soil. Dig in the well-rotted, crumbly compost and you will get very rich soil.

Fertilizer can be used instead of manure or compost but each kind does something different for plants. Get advice from a plant or hardware shop because some kinds are very strong and burn young plants.

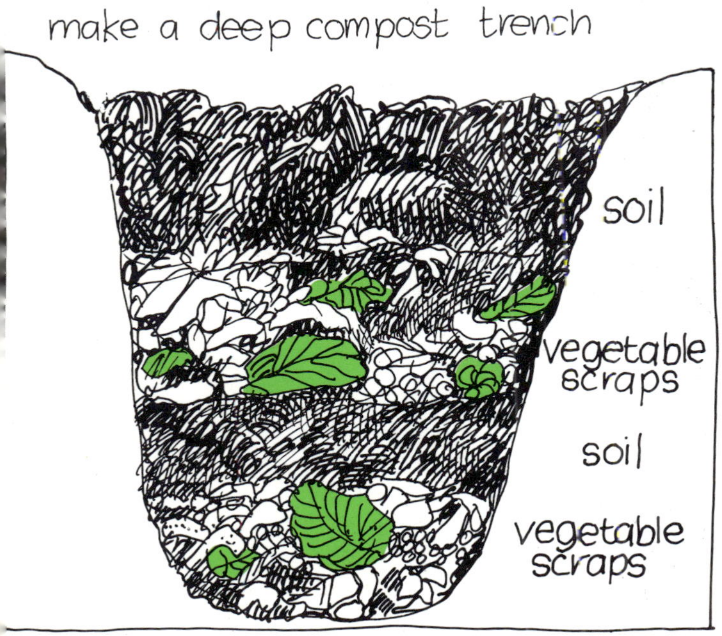

Feeling the soil is the best way to tell if it needs watering. A light sprinkle makes the garden look fresh, but if you stick your fingers into the ground you will find only a thin layer is wet. The roots of most plants go deep so water needs to soak down to reach them.

Pull weeds out often – they use up food and space your plants need.

Bugs will come to eat your plants. Some people spray them with chemicals. This is bad news. Birds that eat poisoned bugs will die and people can get sick, too.

Catch large bugs like caterpillars and snails and feed them to the birds. Smaller bugs can be washed off with slightly soapy water or gently rubbed off with your fingers.

Some plants will grow well in your garden and some won't. Pull out any sick-looking plants and look after the healthy ones. Or try new kinds.

Make sure it is the right time of the year to plant. Some plants need a cool start, others do better when the ground is warm. The back page gives you some ideas about what you could plant now.

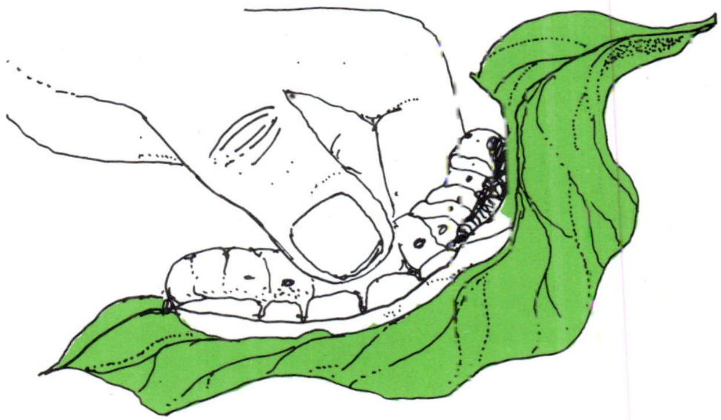

Garden pots

Maybe you have no room for a garden plot or want a private growing place.

You could make a whole garden in a window box, if you have one, or in a collection of pots on a balcony or on a table inside near a window.

Many plants can be grown this way. Climbing beans can grow up a railing, a small tree can grow in a tub outside, or a flower garden can sit on your window sill.

All you need is the right kind of soil, sunshine and lots of containers.

Any kind of tin, bucket and plastic carton can be used as a container. Plastic bottles with their tops cut off work well.

Your pots must have drainage holes in the bottom or the soil will get water-logged. Use a can opener or a hammer and nail.

Put some stones or bits of broken china in the bottom of the pot over the holes. This keeps air gaps around the holes and stops them getting clogged up.

Stand pots in saucers or old lids to catch the water as it seeps through the soil.

Plants growing in pots quickly use up the goodness in the small amount of soil they have to feed on. Potting soil needs to be light and crumbly to let plant roots and water spread through it easily.

The easiest thing to do is to buy a bag of special potting soil mix from a garden shop. This is rich with everything your plants need to grow strong.

Some things will grow in pots of ordinary garden soil. Bulbs, geraniums and water weeds are 3 things you can try if you can't get potting mix.

put stones over drainage holes

Cracks in concrete

In a paved yard you can usually find a few cracks where plants will grow.

Look between bricks and along the edges of walls. Maybe you could lever up one paving stone and make a small garden in its place.

There must be soil in the cracks of course – weeds growing are a good sign. Use a kitchen fork to dig the soil in a small crack.

For sunny cracks where people walk buy a packet of Alyssum seeds. This plant is sometimes called Carpet of Snow. It grows lots of tiny white flowers.

Scatter the seeds in the cracks and gently rake the soil with a fork. Water it lightly.

When the seedlings have 4 leaves each pull some of them out so that the others have room to grow.

Nasturtiums are good for sunny places away from paths. Buy a packet of seeds. Make a hole in the soil with your finger for each one.

Nasturtiums need room to spread and some kinds will climb posts or drainpipes. Tie them up as they grow.

Nasturtium leaves, flowers and seeds can be eaten in sandwiches or salads.

Ivy will grow in the shade. You can find it in many gardens and parks. Pick a healthy piece with new growth and put the stem in a bottle of water until roots appear.

Then plant the ivy in a crack near a wall or pipe. Small clinging roots will grow along the stem as the ivy climbs.

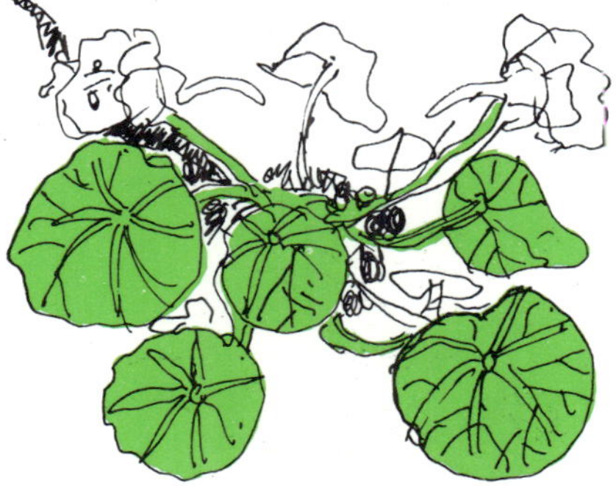

Pumpkins

Pumpkin seeds should be planted in spring or early summer. Buy the seeds in a packet or dry 4 or 5 fat ones from a pumpkin.

Pots won't do for pumpkins which need a great deal of food to grow. So dig a small garden plot over well and mix in some manure if you can.

Make a low mound and poke 4 or 5 seeds around the edge.

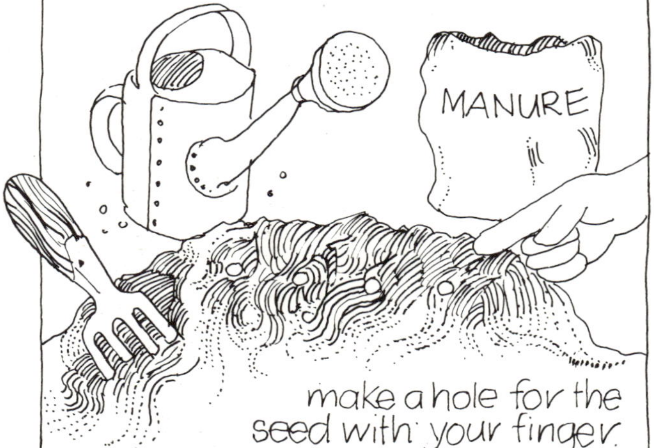

Seedlings should appear after about 2 weeks. Water them every day. Once the vine begins to spread it will grow very fast indeed.

When the flowers form nip off any new tendrils to stop the vine spreading further. This makes the plant stronger and encourages new flowers.

Most of the flowers will be male. Females have the beginnings of pumpkins below their petals. These must be fertilized with pollen from the males or they won't grow.

Watch for bees. They can be seen spreading pollen from the males to the females. Or do it yourself to make sure.

Break off a male flower and rub its pollen-covered stamen gently into the centre of the female flower.

Soon the petals of the female will wither as the small pumpkin starts to swell. The stalk becomes very strong as it carries food to the growing fruit.

Water the roots of the plant every day. It is a good idea now to break off the rest of the flowers so all the strength of the plant goes into producing a few big pumpkins.

A pumpkin is ready to pick when its stalk withers at the end of the summer.

Trees

It is a good feeling to have your own tree. It can be grown in a large tub or planted in a garden.

It is best to buy a young tree in a pot from a plant nursery – maybe you could ask for one for a present.

Trees that have been growing wild or are in another garden may die if they are dug up – or take a long time to grow strong again. Starting your own tree from a seed is a slow and tricky job.

The tree you choose to plant will depend on many things like the climate and the soil where you live.

Work out how much space you have – in a very few years some trees grow tall and spreading. It would be sad to have to chop your tree down.

Visit a plant nursery and talk to someone who can suggest the best kinds of trees to grow in your area. Then choose the one you feel right with.

You might like a fruit tree. An apple tree will grow in almost any garden. Orange trees are good for hot climates.

Once a fruit tree has settled in and grown strong roots and branches, there will be many things to watch. Right through the year you will see changes as the tree blossoms, the fruit swells and ripens, and bugs and birds come.

A cumquat tree grows well in a tub. It has dark shiny leaves and fruit like tiny oranges. These are rather sour but taste good with lots of sugar or honey.

Some trees have always grown in your part of the world. These are called native trees. The rest were brought in from other countries long ago.

If you plant a native tree that flowers, you will find native birds will come to your garden. This is a good thing to do in cities where most native trees have been cut down.

Water the ground around your tree regularly and give it a soaking in hot weather. You could add some fertilizer to the soil at the time of year when the tree is growing new shoots.

Trees in tubs cannot spread their roots in search of food and water as they can in the ground.

Keep the soil damp and add some fertilizer to make it rich. Buy the kind that is right for your tree and read the label first. Too little is better than too much.

Bulbs

Once you have planted bulbs in your garden they will come up every year. New bulbs form under the ground so more and more will flower each spring.

Plant bulbs in the autumn to have flowers at the end of winter or early spring.

If you cut a bulb in half you will find a tiny plant inside. This is fed and protected by the juicy scales of the bulb.

They need deep soil and a fairly sunny place. Plant a few bulbs well under the surface with their noses pointing up.

When the bulbs flower don't pick the leaves. These die after they have finished making the food the buried bulbs need.

Some kinds of bulbs will grow in pots too – like grape hyacinths or daffodils.

Try planting bulbs in potting mixture indoors. The bulbs can be very close together in the pot – almost touching.

Large bulbs should have their noses level with the top of the soil. Smaller bulbs like their tips just covered.

After potting give the bulbs a good soaking. Put them in a cool dark place until leaves appear. Then move them into the light.

Keep the soil damp. Once the leaves are well grown find a warm sunny place near a window for flowering.

Potato

Plant a potato in a large bucket and with any luck you should get a bucketful in about 4 months. Early spring or autumn is the best time.

Any large container will do but it must have drainage holes in the bottom.

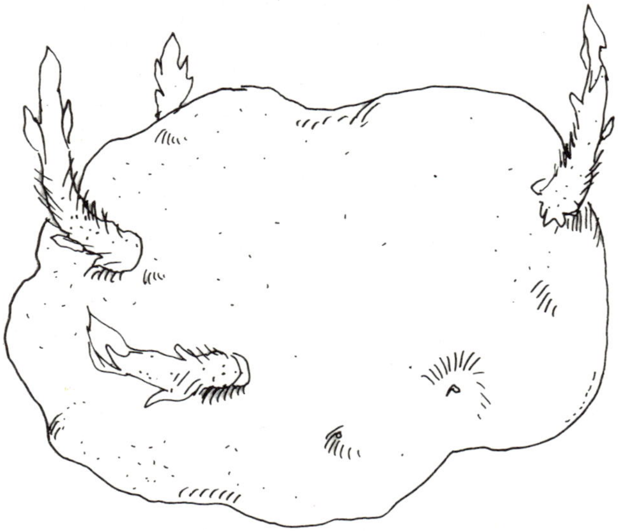

you might find a sprouting potato in the kitchen - or sprout one yourself

Choose a potato with lots of eyes. These are buds and some of them will begin to sprout if the potato is left in a light airy place for about a fortnight.

Half fill your container with soil and mix in a little compost or complete fertilizer.

Make a hole in the soil large enough to take the potato, and cover it over.

In 3 or 4 weeks green shoots will appear above the ground. Now add just enough soil to cover them again. This forces the stem to keep pushing upwards while little potatoes are forming along it below the ground.

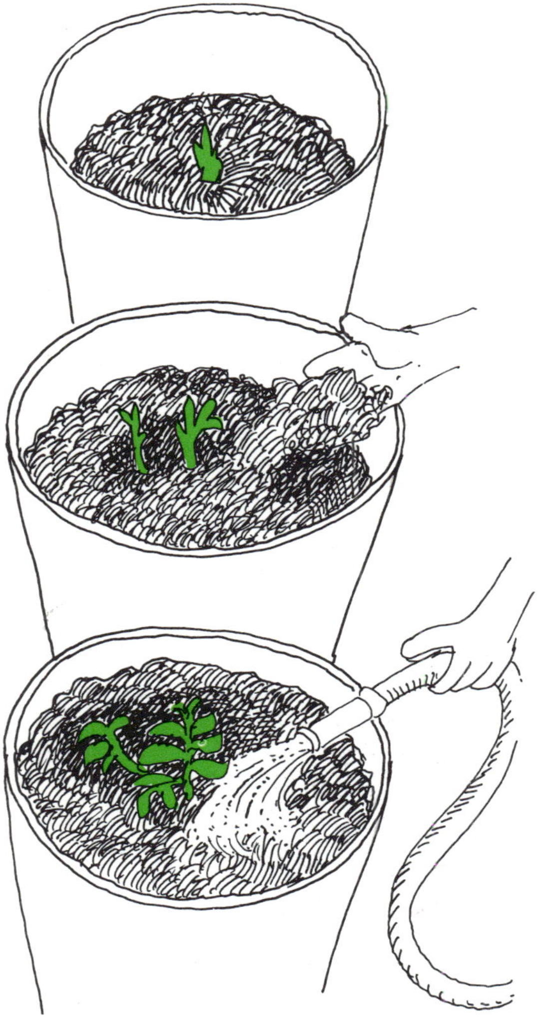

Keep covering the plant until the bucket is full. The soil should be kept damp.

The plant will flower – a sign that things are happening underground. When the flowers die, stop watering. Potatoes will have formed and wetness might make them rot.

When the whole plant dies tip the bucket out and see how many potatoes you have produced.

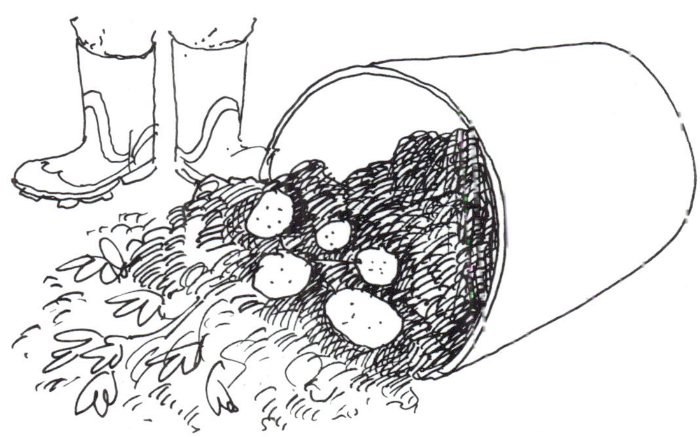

Flower garden

You can make a flower garden in a window box or a collection of pots filled with potting mixture.

In a garden plot flowers and vegetables can grow side by side. Or save a part for a mass of flowers.

Flower seeds or seedlings are usually planted 2 seasons before they blossom. Nemesia seeds planted in autumn will flower in spring. Petunia seedlings planted in spring will flower in summer. Forget-me-knots can be planted at any time of the year in a warm place.

So when you first start flower planting you will have to wait a few months for flowers to bloom.

Keep planting different kinds every few weeks and after the first wait you will have fresh flowers as some die.

You could have flowers all the year round. If the winters are very cold where you live move your garden inside in pots.

Some plants die after flowering – like wallflowers and iceland poppies. You must plant new seeds or seedlings to have more next year.

Others will stay alive after the flowers die and will bloom again year after year – like violets and primroses.

Others die off after scattering their seed. So more will come up somewhere next year – maybe over the fence or in the street. Forget-me-knots and primulas only need planting once.

Buy flower seeds or seedlings from a plant shop.

Get the garden ready by raking it well, or fill your pots with potting mixture.

Plant seedlings as soon as you can after buying them.

Make a hole for each seedling large enough to take the roots without squashing them. Notice where the soil has reached along the stem before – this tells you how deep to plant.

Dangle the roots into the hole and press the soil gently around them. Tip on a cup of water to get rid of air pockets.

If you buy a packet of seeds it will probably tell you how to plant them.

Scatter fine seeds on the soil and cover them with a thin layer of earth. Settle them in with a gentle spray of water.

Large seeds need a hole for each one. Poke your finger halfway into the earth and put in a seed.

Press the soil over it and water each one with a fine spray.

When the small seedlings appear and are growing well, thin them out. Pull up some of the smaller ones to give the others room to grow.

Mushrooms

These are some of the most mysterious things of all to grow.

If you have trouble collecting the things you need, look in the telephone book for mushroom growers in your area.

Heap the manure and straw together and mix it with a fork. If the pile is out in the open cover it with a sack or plastic sheet.

After a few days the pile will feel hot. Turn it over and if it has dried out water it lightly. Do this every few days for about 3 weeks.

The manure mixture is ready when it is brown and crumbly. Pack it firmly into the boxes so they are almost filled.

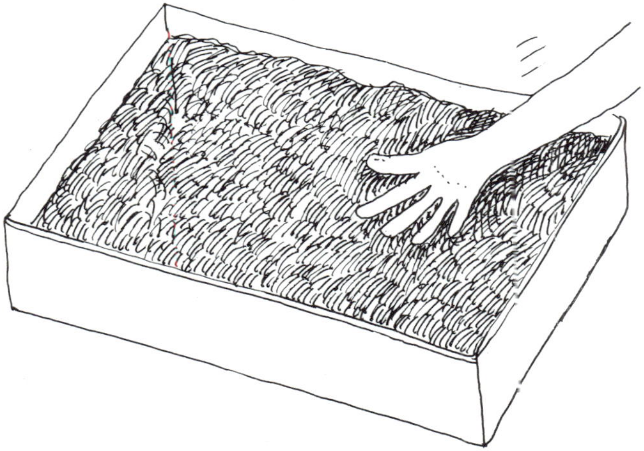

Crumble the mushroom spawn and press it into the surface of the manure.

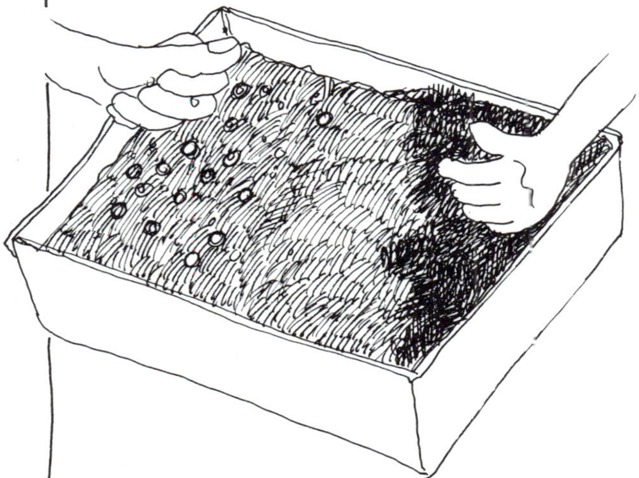

Fill the boxes right up now by covering the manure with a layer of damp garden soil.

Put the boxes in a sheltered place where there are no draughts – under the house, or in a cupboard or shed.

Keep the mushroom beds damp but not wet. Too much water will kill them.

If the weather is not too cold you will see tiny white dots after about 6 weeks. One week later the first mushrooms will be big enough to eat. More and more will appear for several months.

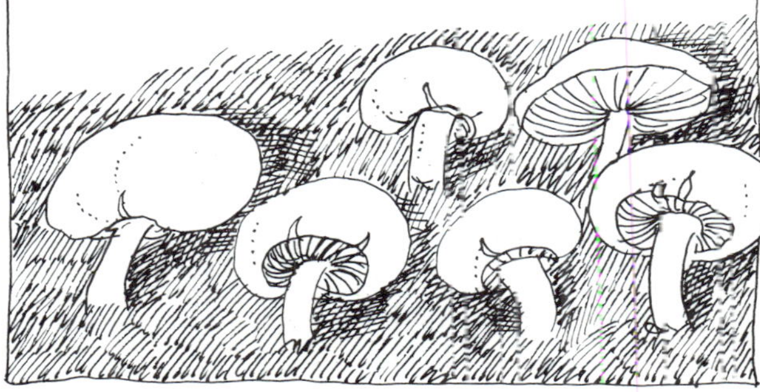

Tomatoes

Home grown tomatoes taste quite different from shop ones. They can be planted in a large pot or in a garden plot. Even 1 plant will give lots of fruit if it is well cared for and gets plenty of sun.

Tomato plants need lots of food. You will need some compost, manure or buy a good tomato fertilizer.

Buy tomato seedlings and plant them in the early spring. You will have tomatoes ready to eat in summer.

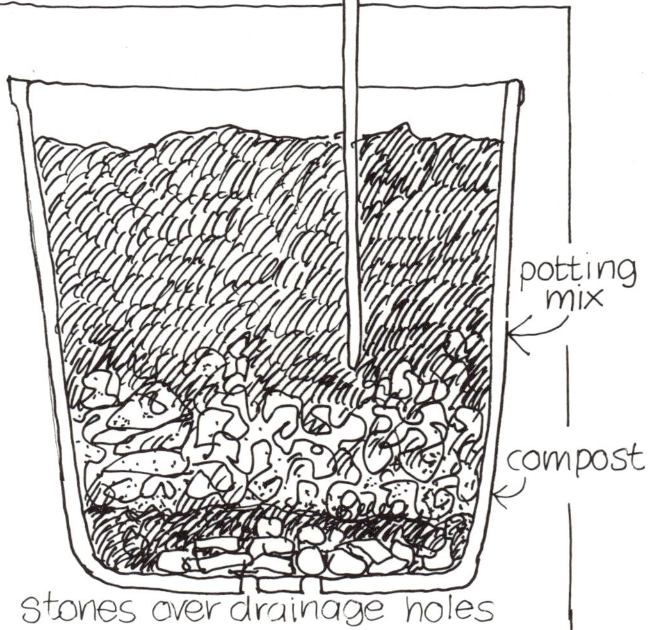

A pot the size of a bucket will be big enough for 1 plant. It grows best in potting mixture with some compost or fertilizer sprinkled in the soil at the bottom of the pot.

If you are growing them in the garden mix the plant food well into the soil before planting.

Put a long strong stake in the pot or ground next to every seedling you plant. Put the seedling quite deep into the earth – nearly up to the first leaves.

The plant will become tall and heavy with fruit. Tie it to the stake as it grows.

You will get more tomatoes from your plant if you save its strength by letting it grow in one direction only.

Watch for shoots that start to grow out where the leaves join the main stem. These are the beginnings of side branches. Pinch them off with your fingers.

The small shoots that will produce flowers and then tomatoes grow straight out of the main stem – don't take these off by mistake.

When the plant reaches the top of the stake stop it getting any taller by pinching off new growth.

Water the soil – not the leaves – often as the plant grows. Pick off any yellow leaves too.

The first tomatoes should ripen about 12 weeks after planting. Pick the fruit as soon as it is turning red to lighten the load on the plant.

At the end of the summer some of the tomatoes may still be green. Pick them and ripen them indoors on a sunny window sill.

Seeds

Seeds are rather like packets of plant food with a tiny plant inside.

The new plant begins to grow when conditions are just right. This usually happens under the ground. But some kinds of seeds only need water to get the message to start sprouting.

You can watch this. Try large seeds – like sunflowers, nasturtiums, beans or wheat – so you can see what happens.

Soak the seeds overnight in water. Then scatter them on a bed of damp cottonwool in a saucer.

Keep the cottonwool damp and in a few days you will see the seeds begin to sprout. Watch for the start of roots and then a stem

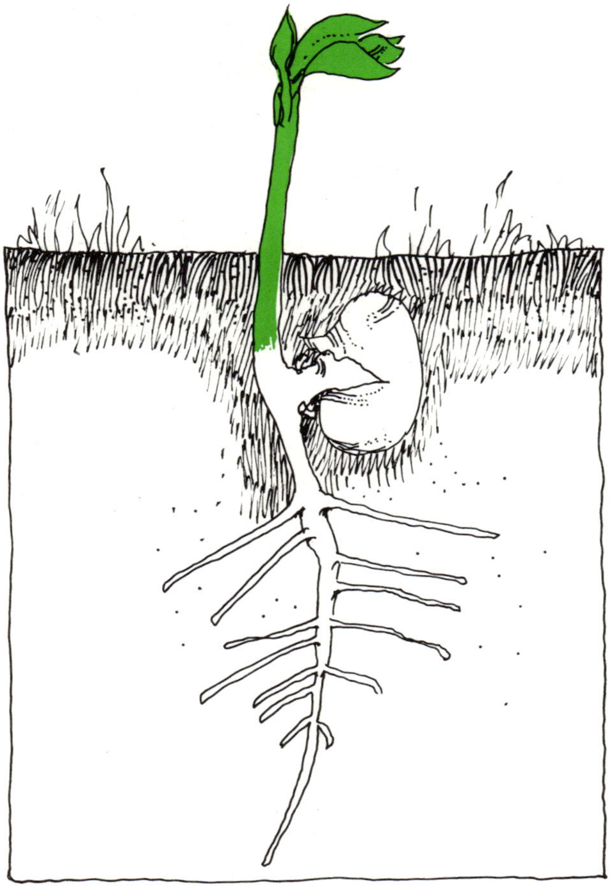

put the saucer on a sunny window sill

bean shoots grown like this are good to eat

Try growing strange little trees from fruit pips. They won't be very like the tree the fruit came from. Fruit trees have been made the way they are by people – your pips will sprout in their own way.

Orange or grapefruit pips are easier to grow than pips with very hard cases – like cherries or plums. But try them anyway.

Choose pips that are fat and come from ripe fruit. Nothing will grow if it has been cooked first.

You will need a collection of small containers with potting mix in them.

Soak the pips overnight in water. Then plant several of the same kind of seed in each pot because some won't grow.

A seed that falls to the ground in ripe fruit from a tree won't sprout until next year. You are going to speed things up.

Put the pots in a warm dark place and water them every day.

When shoots appear above the soil you can keep them growing indoors on a sunny window sill. You might get several seeds sprouting in one pot. Pull out all but the strongest one.

You could gather seeds from trees that bear fruit we don't eat too. Acorns will sprout quite easily if you collect them when they are ripe and have fallen from the tree.

Sunflowers

Sunflowers are easy to grow in a sunny place and some kinds will grow much taller than you. Plant them in the spring.

Scatter a whole packet of seeds over part of your garden plot and cover them lightly with soil.

Water them as they grow. When the seedlings appear pull some of them up so the others have enough room.

Sunflowers grow quite fast and may need to be tied to stakes if they are in a windy place.

When the plant has flowered and begins to wither, you can gather lots of dark shiny seeds from the centre of the flower.

Pull the plant out and cut off the flower head. Rub the seeds out with a rake or garden fork.

Keep some seeds in a paper bag for planting next year. Dry some in the oven to eat and give some away. Feed some to the birds in winter when food is scarce.

Climbing beans

Beans grow well in a small garden bed or a pot. They should be planted in spring or summer. Climbing beans take up very little space.

Beans dried for cooking won't sprout – so buy a packet of seeds from a garden shop.

You could plant 3 climbing bean seeds in a bucket-sized pot.

Before planting the beans in a garden or a pot make a frame for them to climb on. Use 3 or 4 long sticks – taller than you. Stick them well into the ground and tie the tops into a wigwam shape.

Plant the seeds next to the sticks. In a garden bed 2 beans could climb up each stick.

While you are waiting for the plants to come up you could put 1 or 2 seeds on a saucer of damp cotton wool inside. You will be able to watch the beans sprout as they are doing under the ground.

As soon as the plants are long enough, start to twist the stems around the sticks.

When the beans reach the top of the sticks, pinch off the tips of the new shoots.

Water the plants well as they grow – every day in dry weather. Watch for weeds and pull them out.

The beans will be ready to pick in about 12 weeks. Leave a few to dry on the plant and collect bean seeds for next year.

Water garden

A water garden can be made in a container the size of a baby's bath or an old laundry tub. It can stand on a balcony or perhaps be sunk into the ground in a garden. Find a sunny sheltered spot as water plants grow best in water warmed by the sun.

Put a layer of garden soil about 10 cm deep in the bottom of the tub and fill it with water.

You can buy water weeds, water snails and small fish in most pet shops. Or look for wild weeds in freshwater places.

Put a small stone on the water weed to stop it floating to the surface. It will grow new roots quickly to anchor it into the soil.

Water lilies can be bought in pots. Choose dwarf or pigmy lilies for a small tub.

Just stand the pot under the water. The lily will grow up to float its leaves and flowers on the surface.

The plants and animals living in water gardens keep the water clean and each other healthy.

Water weeds put oxygen into the water for the snails and fish to breathe

water snails and fish fertilize the soil with their droppings. they breathe out carbon dioxide for the plants to use

Geraniums

Geraniums can be grown indoors in a pot or in a sunny garden. There are many different kinds and colours.

One of the good things about geraniums is that they grow from cuttings. This means you don't have to wait a long time before you have a plant.

Many gardens have geraniums growing so look around and ask for a cutting. This is a small piece of the plant that has a healthy sprouting shoot on it. No root is needed because the cutting very quickly grows more when it is stuck in the soil.

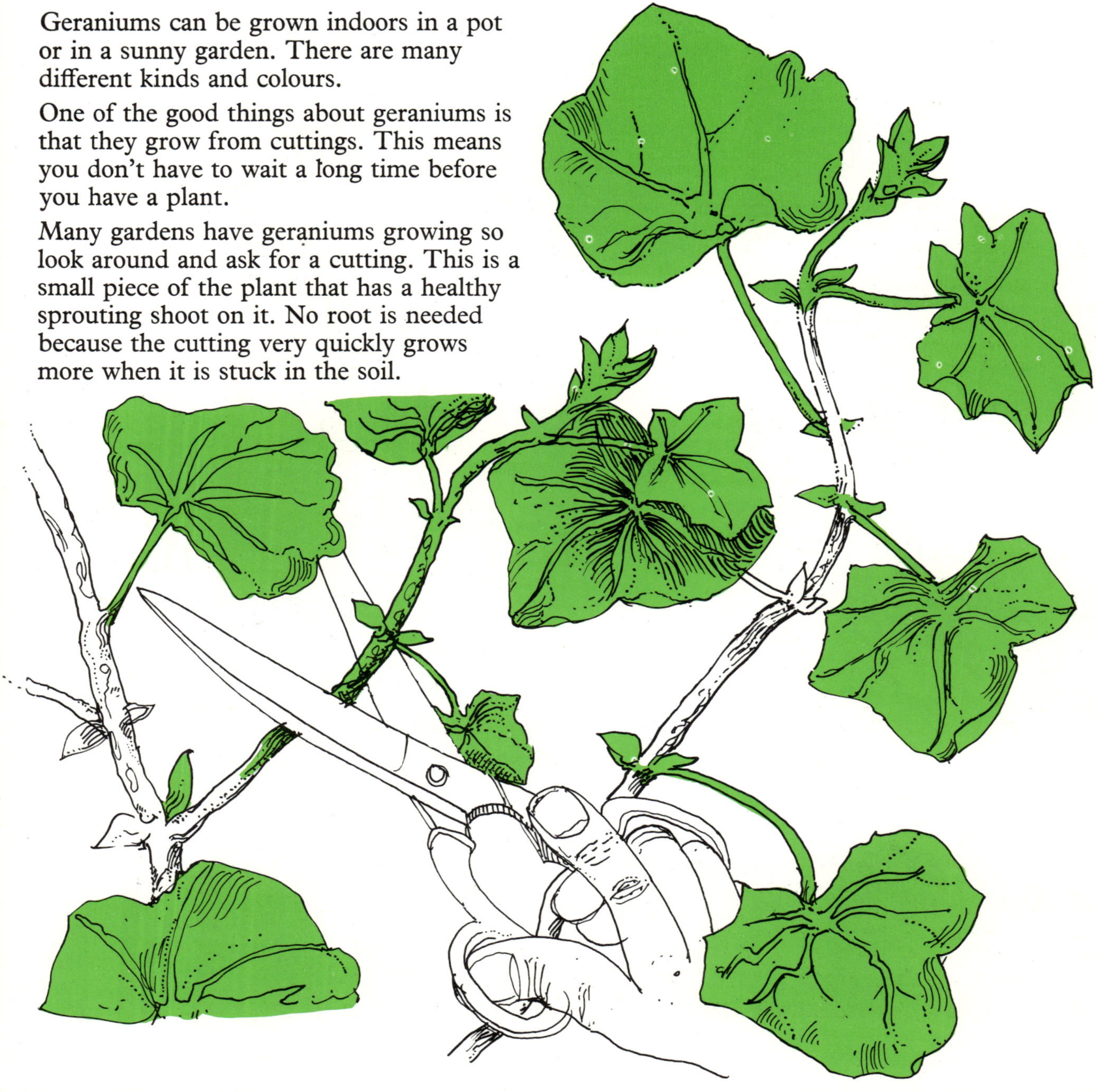

Keep the soil around the plant damp. If the plant becomes a straggly shape pinch off some of the untidy shoots from time to time.

If you have a geranium in a pot indoors put it near a window where the sun will reach it for at least part of the day.

You will notice that the flowers always turn towards the light outside. Turn the pot around and the flowers will turn back to face the window.

Calendar

At different times of the year you can grow different things. In some places it is warm all year round and plants will grow well at any time. In places where the ground freezes in winter you will have to wait for warmer weather to garden outdoors. But gardens in pots will grow at any time in a warm room. Check with a garden shop to see what you can plant now in your part of the world.

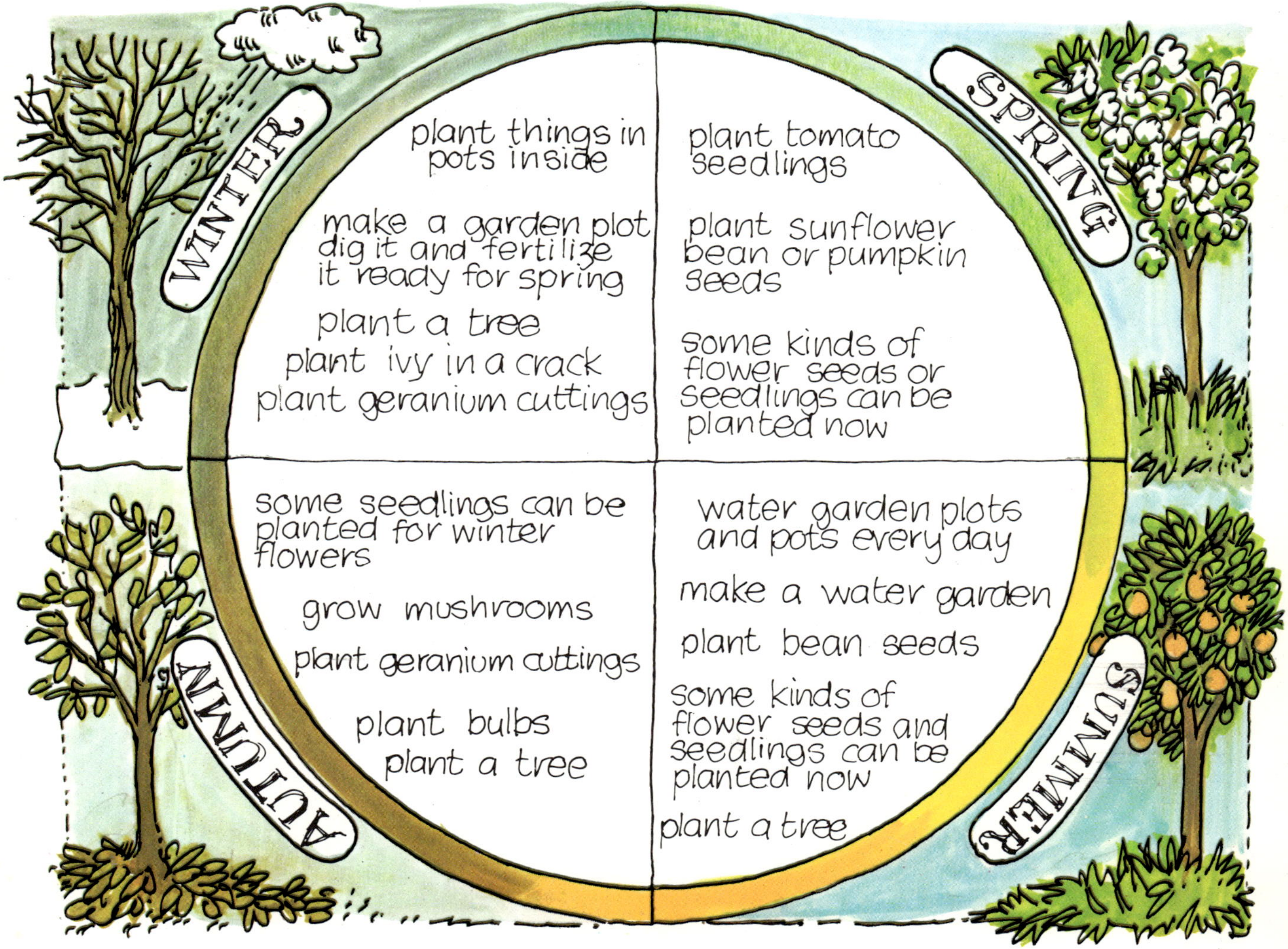